REAL-LIFE
DRAGONS

EDGE
BOOKS

BEARDED DRAGONS

by Wil Mara

Consultant:
Colin Donihue, PhD
Postdoctoral Researcher
Department of Organismic and Evolutionary Biology
Harvard University
Cambridge, Massachusetts

CAPSTONE PRESS
a capstone imprint

Edge Books are published by Capstone Press,
1710 Roe Crest Drive, North Mankato, Minnesota 56003
www.mycapstone.com

Library of Congress Cataloging-in-Publication Data
Cataloging-in-Publication Data is on file at the Library of Congress website.
ISBN 978-1-5157-5070-3 (library binding)
ISBN 978-1-5157-5074-1 (paperback)
ISBN 978-1-5157-5086-4 (eBook PDF)
Summary: Discusses the behavior, habitat, and life cycle of bearded dragons.

Editorial Credits
Abby Colich, editor; Bobbie Nuytten, designer; Pam Mitsakos, media researcher;
Steve Walker, production specialist

Image Credits
Getty Images: Carl Court, 26; iStockphoto: Wesley Tolhurst, 14; Minden Pictures:
Neil Bowman/FPLA, 25, Robert Valentic/NPL, 6-7; Science Source: ANT Photo
Library, 21; Shutterstock: BLFootage, 16-17, Camilo Torres, 4, Cat Downie,
8, Eric Isselee, 28, FiledIMAGE, 19, gracethang2, 11, ifong, 12 bottom right,
Janelle Lugge, 18, mark Higgins, 10, Matt McClain, 13, reptiles4all, 9, Sirichai
Puangsuwan, 24, Skripnikova E, 5, small1, 12 bottom left, valleyboi63, cover
right, wavebreakmedia, 27; Thinkstock: chat9780, 15, VittoriaChe, 23

Design Elements:
Shutterstock: Andrii_M, iulias, Limbad, yyang

Printed and bound in the USA.
10028S17CG

TABLE OF CONTENTS

CHAPTER 1
A CREEPING DRAGON 4

CHAPTER 2
BEARDED DRAGON HOMES 10

CHAPTER 3
BUILT LIKE A DRAGON 12

CHAPTER 4
BEHAVING LIKE DRAGONS 14

CHAPTER 5
MEAL TIME 16

CHAPTER 6
FROM EGG TO ADULT 20

CHAPTER 7
PROTECTING BEARDED DRAGONS 24

BEARDED DRAGON FACTS 28
GLOSSARY 30
READ MORE 31
INTERNET SITES 31
CRITICAL THINKING USING THE
     COMMON CORE 32
INDEX 32

A CREEPING DRAGON

It's sunset in the desert. A creature scurries across the sand. Then it hears something. The creature slows down and turns. Without a sound, it creeps onto a rock. A bug scuttles along below. The creature does not care what kind of bug this is. Food isn't easy to find in the desert. The creature moves down the other side of the rock, slowly. It gets within inches of the bug. It lunges forward with its mouth open. Bam! It snatches the meal off the ground.

The **prey** struggles to free itself. But the creature's grip is too tight. Its **venom** is too strong. Soon the bug stops wiggling. The creature swallows it in a few mighty gulps. Then it licks the last lingering flavors from around its mouth and moves on. This creature is a bearded dragon lizard. It is still hungry. There is more hunting to do.

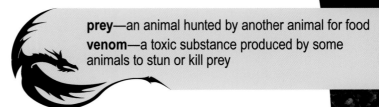

prey—an animal hunted by another animal for food
venom—a toxic substance produced by some animals to stun or kill prey

The Dragons of Mythology

Lizards that are called "dragons" get their name from the dragons of myth. The word "dragon" comes from Latin and Greek words that mean "huge serpent." Dragons of stories are giant, fire-breathing beasts. They often have spiked tails and scaly skin. Bearded dragons have some things in common with the dragons of lore. Their skin is scaly. They have long tails. Fortunately, bearded dragons don't breathe fire!

A SPIKY DRAGON

The bearded dragon is an interesting lizard. Its body is wide and flat. Little spikes run around its triangular head. It has a flap of skin on its throat. The flap extends when the animal is angry or alarmed. A male also pushes out the flap when trying to attract females. When the flap extends, it turns a dark color. It looks like a beard. This is how the lizard gets the "bearded" part of its name.

A bearded dragon's mouth is wide and thin. A narrow, pink tongue helps it grab food. More rows of spikes run along its sides between the front and hind legs. It has five long claws on each foot. Its long tail sweeps back and forth in the sand.

A bearded dragon's pebbly skin is brown, gray, or tan. Darker spots may run along the back and down the tail. Its belly is lighter, usually yellow, cream, or white. Males are able to change color. They can become darker during fights with other males.

Male bearded dragons are slightly larger than females. They average about 22 to 24 inches (56 to 61 centimeters) long. Females grow to about 18 to 20 inches (46 to 51 cm) long.

The "beard" on this dragon became darker as it extended out from its neck.

IDENTIFYING DRAGONS

The bearded dragon is a reptile. Scales cover a reptile's body. The scales are tough and dry. The bearded dragon is a type of reptile called a lizard. The bearded dragon is part of a group of lizards known as agamids. Agamid lizards have strong legs. They are excellent climbers. They also have triangular-shaped heads. Many agamid lizards can also change color.

The Sinai agama is an agamid lizard related to the bearded dragon.

Within the agamids, the bearded dragon is in a group called *Pogona*. *Pogona* includes all the known **species** of bearded dragons. There are eight *Pogona* species. Each species looks slightly different from the others.

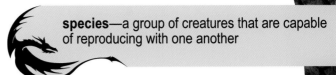

species—a group of creatures that are capable of reproducing with one another

Rankin's dragon is a rare species found only in northeastern Australia.

DRAGON FACT

Of the eight species of *Pogona*, the eastern bearded dragon was discovered first, in 1829. The most recent, Rankin's dragon, was first identified in 1985.

CHAPTER 2

BEARDED DRAGON HOMES

Bearded dragons live throughout much of Australia. They are found in areas that are dry and hot, such as deserts. These lizards can withstand temperatures up to 100 degrees Fahrenheit (37.7 degrees Celsius). But they like it in the 80 to 90°F (26.6 to 32.2°C) range.

Bearded dragons spend most of their time off the ground. They like to climb trees, shrubs, and rocks. They come to the ground to hunt for food. If the temperature becomes unbearably high, they may look for holes in which to **burrow**. Females will also come to the ground to lay eggs.

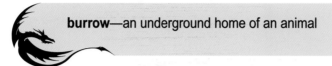

burrow—an underground home of an animal

Bearded dragons live in dry land with trees and shrubs, such as this area in Australia.

Dragons All Over

Different species of *Pogona* live in different areas. Some cover larger areas than others. The central bearded dragon, for example, lives throughout central, eastern, and southern Australia. The Drysdale River bearded dragon lives only in a small section of the northwest. The ranges of these two species do not overlap. They will never see each other!

This eastern bearded dragon lives in wooded areas in the eastern part of Australia.

CHAPTER 3

BUILT LIKE A DRAGON

Bearded dragons have certain features that help them survive. Their claws are sharp. The claws help them easily move up and down trees and shrubs. Their tough skin holds water. This keeps them from getting dried out in the brutal desert heat. Their eyes have eyelids. Eyelids protect their eyes from harsh sunlight. They also shield the eyes from clouds of sand that roll over them when the wind blows.

sharp claws

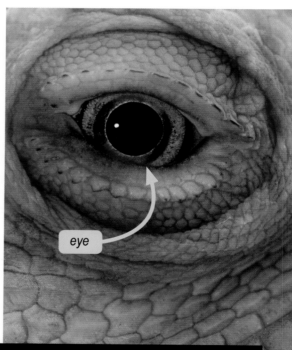

eye

DRAGON FACT

Bearded dragons absorb vitamins from the sun into their skin. Vitamin D helps with important bodily functions such as proper growth of teeth and bones. The same is true for humans!

The spikes on numerous parts of their body are not sharp at all. They are soft and rubbery. **Predators**, however, don't know this! An animal that might want to make a meal out of a bearded dragon sees these dangerous-looking spikes. It thinks twice before attacking.

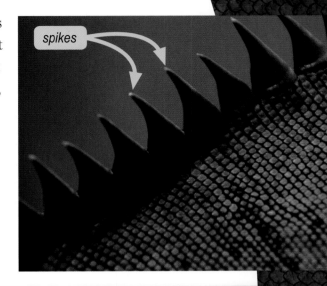

spikes

Staying Warm

Like all reptiles, bearded dragons are *cold-blooded*. Their bodies can't stay warm on their own. They rely on heat sources in their habitat. They lie on rocks that have been warmed by the sun. This warms their bellies. The heat from the sun warms their backs.

predator—an animal that hunts another animal for food
cold-blooded—having a body that needs to get heat from its surroundings

CHAPTER 4

BEHAVING LIKE DRAGONS

Bearded dragons are **solitary** creatures. They spend most of their time alone. They are also very **territorial**. A bearded dragon chooses an area as its own. If another bearded dragon crosses into it, the dragon gets very huffy. It inflates its "beard"— the loose flap of skin under the throat. It puffs it out until it looks like a spiny balloon. The "beard" turns a dark color, often black. The lizard may also open its mouth to show off its long rows of sharp teeth.

This angry bearded dragon has puffed out the flap of skin under his throat. The flap has also darkened.

Bearded dragons also bob their heads up and down. This is a sign to others that they are the **dominant** lizard in the territory. They may also inflate their torsos. They fill their lungs with air. Then they let it out slowly through their mouths. This creates a hissing noise. Tail-twitching is also a sign of anger and stress.

If a bearded dragon feels it has no other choice, it will attack an invader. It claws and bites to drive the invader away. Sometimes males that are large and dominant will lie on top of smaller males that refuse to leave their territory.

solitary—living and hunting alone
territorial—defending an area of land as one's own
dominant—the most powerful or important

DRAGON FACT

Male bearded dragons tend to be the most territorial. But females exhibit a bit of this behavior too. Both male and female adults are much more territorial than young bearded dragons.

CHAPTER 5
MEAL TIME

Bearded dragons spend most of their time searching for their next meal. They are active mostly during the day. They may hunt during twilight hours if daytime becomes too hot. Some may also hunt at night. The cool air draws out more prey.

Bearded dragons are **omnivores**. They eat both plants and animals. In the desert, food can be scarce. So bearded dragons aren't picky. They eat tiny insects such beetles, ants, crickets, and cockroaches. They also enjoy small rodents or reptiles, including other lizards. When it comes to plants, they will happily munch on leafy greens that hang from trees and shrubs.

A bearded dragon's tongue makes a sticky fluid that helps it hold its prey. A bearded dragon also produces venom. They use the venom to subdue insects that won't stay still after being caught!

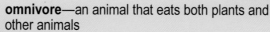

omnivore—an animal that eats both plants and other animals

This bearded dragon has caught a large, winged insect for its meal.

DRAGON FACT

Young bearded dragons eat more
insects than plants. Adults get half their
food from plants. They get the other half
from animals.

WATER FOR DRAGONS

Getting enough water in the desert isn't easy. Bearded dragons drink it wherever they can find it. If a puddle or small stream is not close by, they lick moisture off leaves or other surfaces. Some species have special scales that funnel dew and water from wet sand. The water runs over their bodies and into their mouths.

HUNTED DRAGONS

Bearded dragons sometimes become prey for other animals. Predators include large birds such as eagles, hawks, and falcons. Bigger lizards prey on them as well. One such lizard is the perentie. The perentie is one of the largest lizards in the world. Pythons also prey on bearded dragons. Dingoes, wild dogs that eat just about anything, include bearded dragons in their diet.

The huge perentie lizard hunts and eats bearded dragons.

The wild Australian dog known as the dingo is a major predator of bearded dragons.

DRAGON DEFENSES

Bearded dragon venom is only strong enough to hurt the dragons' prey. They don't use it to defend themselves from predators. Their most common type of defense is scurrying off to the nearest hiding place. Otherwise, they may claw or bite.

CHAPTER 6

FROM EGG TO ADULT

Bearded dragons **mate** once a year, usually in the springtime. They begin mating at about one or two years old.

During mating season, males become **aggressive** toward each other. This behavior is most intense when two males want the same female. Males will bob their heads at each other. They inflate their "beards." They open their mouths and hiss. They may even scratch and bite one another. Eventually, a dominant male wins a female. He may do more head bobbing and beard spreading in front of the female. If the female is interested, she will often raise one of her front claws and move it around.

About a month after mating, the female digs a hole in the ground. She lays 10 to 30 eggs. The oblong eggs are about 1 inch (2.5 cm) in length. Then she covers the eggs with dirt to protect them. She does not come back to check on the eggs. The eggs hatch two to three months later.

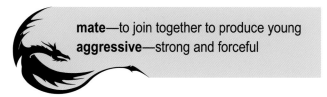

mate—to join together to produce young
aggressive—strong and forceful

Bearded dragons hatch from eggs and climb out of their underground nest.

DRAGON FACT

Sometimes a predator digs up and eats bearded dragon eggs before they hatch.

GROWING UP DRAGON

Tiny bearded dragons hatch from eggs. The hatchlings are about 3 to 4 inches (7.6 to 10.2 cm) long. Baby dragons have much brighter markings than adults. They are light tan or gray with very dark markings. The markings fade over time.

Bearded dragons are on their own from the time the eggs are laid. Once they hatch, they begin hunting almost immediately. They also search for a good hiding place. Predators eat many of them. Bearded dragons know the importance of staying alert.

At about one year old, bearded dragons reach adulthood. The average bearded dragon lives about five years in the wild.

DRAGON FACT

Younger or smaller males may lift one of their front claws and move it in a circular motion. This shows that they are *submissive* and not a threat.

submissive—not having power or control

young bearded dragon

23

CHAPTER 7

PROTECTING BEARDED DRAGONS

As with many wild animals, the bearded dragon faces several threats. Some species are plentiful in the wild. Others face issues such as illegal pet trades and habitat destruction.

ILLEGAL PET TRADE

Bearded dragons are popular pets. They are small and don't need a lot of space. They are easy to feed. Most bearded dragons sold in pet stores are **bred** in captivity. These are legal to buy and sell. It is illegal to capture wild bearded dragons and then sell them. Every female caught reduces the number of young that will be born in the wild. This could cause the wild population to decline. This is especially true for species that occur in very small numbers and in small areas.

HABITAT DESTRUCTION

One main threat to bearded dragons is habitat destruction. Their fragile homes in Australia are increasingly being bulldozed. New buildings are developed in these places. When they lose their homes, bearded dragons can no longer survive or reproduce. Many other species are at risk for the same reason.

breed—to mate and raise a certain kind of animal

When land is cleared for development, the wildlife in that area no longer have a place to live.

HOPE FOR DRAGONS

Scientists breed some bearded dragon species in captivity. They hope to introduce the offspring into the wild. Lawmakers are introducing policies that protect and preserve certain habitats. With these efforts, bearded dragons may have a chance to survive well into the future.

An animal rescue worker feeds a bearded dragon in Brighton, England.

You Can Help Too

You might not live near any bearded-dragon habitats. But you can still play a role in preserving nature. Don't throw your trash anywhere except in a trash can. Plant new *native* shrubs and trees in areas where others have been cut down or destroyed. Trees and shrubs provide hiding places and homes for many animals. When you venture into a wild place, treat it gently. Leave it exactly as you found it. You might not call the forest home, but thousands of other living things do!

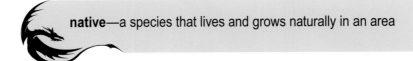

native—a species that lives and grows naturally in an area

BEARDED DRAGON FACTS

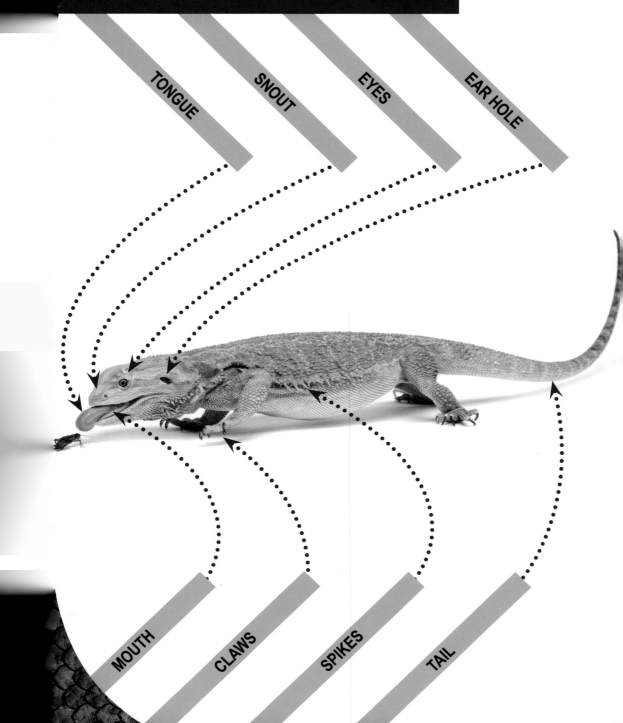

TONGUE

SNOUT

EYES

EAR HOLE

MOUTH

CLAWS

SPIKES

TAIL

NAMES:

Common name: bearded dragon

Genus name: *Pogona* (all bearded dragons)

SPECIES:

coastal or eastern bearded dragon (*Pogona barbata*)

Rankin's dragon (*Pogona henrylawsoni*)

Drysdale River bearded dragon (*Pogona microlepidota*)

Abrolhos or Abrolhos dwarf bearded dragon
   (*Pogona minor minima*)

western bearded dragon (*Pogona minor*)

Mitchell's bearded dragon (*Pogona mitchelli*)

Nullabor bearded dragon (*Pogona nullarbor*)

central or inland bearded dragon (*Pogona vitticeps*)

RANGE:

throughout Australia, except some parts of the extreme north

HABITAT:

dry, arid, rocky, but with enough trees and shrubs to provide
suitable cover

SIZE:

Males are about 22 to 24 inches (56 to 61 cm) long. Females
are about 18 to 20 inches (46 to 51 cm) long.

COLOR:

usually light gray or tan with darker markings, such as brown
or black, with a pale or light belly

PREDATORS:

large birds of prey, dingoes, snakes, larger lizards, humans

LIFESPAN:

around five years in the wild, slightly longer in captivity

GLOSSARY

aggressive (uh-GREH-siv)—strong and forceful

breed (BREED)—to mate and raise a certain kind of animal

burrow (BUHR-oh)—an underground home of an animal

cold-blooded (KOHLD-BLUHD-id)—having a body that needs to get heat from its surroundings

dominant (DAH-muh-nuhnt)—the most powerful or important

mate (MATE)—to join together to produce young

native (NAY-tuhv)—a species that lives and grows naturally in an area

omnivore (OM-nuh-vor)—an animal that eats both plants and other animals

predator (PRED-uh-tur)—an animal that hunts another animal for food

prey (PRAY)—an animal hunted by another animal for food

solitary (SOL-uh-ter-ee)—living and hunting alone

species (SPEE-sheez)—a group of creatures that are capable of reproducing with one another

submissive (suhb-MISS-uhv)—not having power or control

territorial (tare-uh-TOR-ee-uhl)—defending an area of land as one's own

venom (VEN-uhm)—a toxic substance produced by some animals to stun or kill prey

READ MORE

De la Bédoyère, Camilla. *The Wild Life of Lizards.* The Wild Side. New York: Windmill Books, 2015.

Raum, Elizabeth. *Bearded Dragons.* Lizards. Mankato, Minn.: Amicus High Interest, 2015.

Shaffer, Jody Jensen. *Bearded Dragons.* Amazing Reptiles. Minneapolis: Core Library, 2015.

INTERNET SITES

FactHound offers a safe, fun way to find Internet sites related to this book. All of the sites on FactHound have been researched by our staff.

Here's all you do:

Visit *www.facthound.com*

Type in this code: 9781515750703

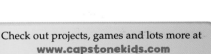

Super-cool stuff! Check out projects, games and lots more at www.capstonekids.com

CRITICAL THINKING USING THE COMMON CORE

1. When are bearded dragons most active? Why do you think this is? What are the advantages? (Craft and Structure)

2. Bearded dragons eat both plants and animals. Why do they need to eat both kinds of food? (Key Idea and Details)

3. Describe where bearded dragons live. Do you think they could survive in other areas of the wild? Explain why or why not. (Integration of Knowledge and Ideas)

INDEX

burrowing, 10

claws, 12, 20
colors, 6, 8, 22

defenses, 19
dragons (myth), 5
drinking, 18

eggs, 10, 20, 21, 22
eyes, 12

food, 16, 17

head bobbing, 15, 20
hunting, 4–5, 10, 16, 22

legs, 6, 8

mating, 20
mouths, 6, 14, 18

predators, 13, 18, 21
prey, 5, 18

scales, 5, 8, 18
size, 7
skin flap ("beard"), 6, 14, 20
species, 9
  central bearded dragon, 11
  Drysdale River bearded dragon, 11
  eastern bearded dragon, 9
  Rankin's dragon, 9
spikes, 6, 13

tails, 5, 6, 15
teeth, 14
territories, 14, 15
threats, 24
  habitat destruction, 25
  illegal pet trade, 24
tongues, 6, 16

venom, 5, 16, 19